THE SUN & MOON SIGNS LIBRARY

SCORPIO

24 OCTOBER – 22 NOVEMBER

JULIA AND DEREK PARKER

Photography by Monique le Luhandre
Illustrations by Danuta Mayer

DORLING KINDERSLEY
London • New York • Stuttgart

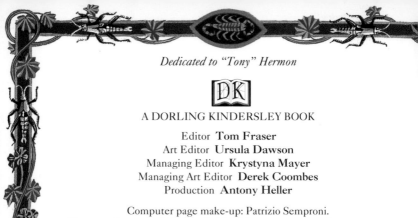

Dedicated to "Tony" Hermon

A DORLING KINDERSLEY BOOK

Editor **Tom Fraser**
Art Editor **Ursula Dawson**
Managing Editor **Krystyna Mayer**
Managing Art Editor **Derek Coombes**
Production **Antony Heller**

Computer page make-up: Patrizio Semproni.
Photography: p 10 CM Dixon/British Museum; p 11 CM Dixon/British
Museum; p 16 Tim Ridley. Stylist: pp 28-29 Lucy Elworthy. Illustration:
pp 60-61 Kuo Kang Chen. Jacket illustration: Peter Lawman.
With thanks to Carolyn Lancaster and John Filbey.

First published in Great Britain in 1992 by
Dorling Kindersley Limited, London WC2E 8PS

A CIP catalogue record for this book is available
from the British Library

ISBN 0-86318-851-6

Reproduced by GRB Editrice, Verona, Italy
Printed and bound in Hong Kong by Imago

CONTENTS

SCORPIO

SCORPIO, THE EIGHTH SIGN OF THE ZODIAC, IS A SIGN OF THE
WATER ELEMENT. IT BESTOWS ON ITS SUBJECTS DEEP,
PENETRATING, AND INTENSE PERSONALITIES, AND GIVES THEM
GREAT RESOURCES OF EMOTIONAL AND PHYSICAL ENERGY.

The qualities of Scorpio must be channelled positively to prevent jealousy and resentfulness from leading to inner dissatisfaction that can badly mar its subjects' characters.

Scorpio has the reputation for being the sexiest of the 12 Zodiac signs. Like most popular astrological beliefs, this is often unjustified. Scorpios need sexual fulfilment, but their energy can also be expressed in many other ways.

Pluto, the sign's ruling planet, underlines a characteristic sense of purpose. For Scorpios to be psychologically fulfilled, every single day must have its own full and demanding schedule.

Traditional groupings

As you read through this book you will come across references to the elements and the qualities, and to positive and negative, or masculine and feminine signs. The first grouping, the elements, comprises fire, earth, air, and water signs. The second, the qualities, divides the Zodiac into cardinal, fixed, and mutable signs. The final grouping consists of positive and negative, or masculine and feminine signs. Each Zodiac sign is associated with a combination of components from these groupings, all of which add different characteristics to it.

Scorpio characteristics

The sign is of the fixed quality, which indicates stubbornness; something of a contradiction in terms when one thinks of the ebb and flow of water, the Scorpio element. The sign is also feminine and negative, which signifies introversion. There is a traditional association between Scorpio and dramatic, deep shades of red and maroon.

Scorpios often have incisive minds and a great desire to get to the bottom of every problem.

ARIES PISCES AQUARIUS CAPRICORN SAGITTARIUS SCORPIO LIBRA VIRGO LEO CANCER GEMINI TAURUS

FIRE

CARDINAL EARTH

MASCULINE MUTABLE AIR

FEMININE FIXED WATER

The Zodiac Wheel

The relationship between each Zodiac sign and the traditional astrological groupings is made clear within the Zodiac wheel. As you read through this book you will also discover references to polar, or opposite signs, and these, too, can be easily worked out by referring to the wheel.

MYTHS & LEGENDS

THE ZODIAC, WHICH IS SAID TO HAVE ORIGINATED IN
BABYLON AS LONG AS 2,500 YEARS AGO, IS
A CIRCLE OF CONSTELLATIONS THROUGH WHICH THE SUN
MOVES DURING THE COURSE OF A YEAR.

Fairly often, it takes a very great leap of the imagination to see any definite likeness between the "shape" of some constellations and the different Zodiac symbols that have come to be associated with them. A case does, perhaps, exist for saying that the constellation of Scorpio has a tail that resembles a scorpion's. In the case of Scorpio, however, the obscure link between its Zodiac symbol and the pattern in the stars that constitutes the Scorpio constellation is quite hard to explain.

Evidence suggests that the Scorpio symbol initially had no link with a constellation. A scorpion-man, apparently not based on any group of stars, appears as a fully developed

Orion the hunter
This image, cut into the back of an Etruscan mirror, shows Orion crossing the sea.

image on many Babylonian boundary stones. On the majority of these boundary stones, he is depicted with a scorpion's tail, and drawing a bow, as though he were a combination of the figures for Scorpio and Sagittarius, the Archer. This scorpion figure appeared in Babylon at least 1,000 years before he finally took his place in the Egyptian Zodiacs that were created in the ancient cities of Denderah and Esna, as the image we know today.

Orion and Eos
Manilius, the Roman writer who, in the first century B.C., set down several astrological myths, suggested that the original scorpion was

connected with Orion. A Greek giant (it was said that his stature was so great that he could walk on the bottom of the sea without getting his head wet), hunter, and the handsomest man alive, he was by no means impervious to female charms.

When the dawn-goddess Eos, an inveterate collector of handsome young men, invited him to bed, he happily accepted the invitation. But Orion bragged of the conquest, and also boasted that he was so great a hunter that he would exterminate all of the wild beasts.

The god Apollo, responsible for guarding herds, therefore persuaded Gaia, the Earth goddess, to send a giant scorpion with impenetrable armour to sting him to death.

Artemis's mistake

Some variations of this myth say that it succeeded, others that Orion tried to escape by swimming out to sea, only to be accidentally shot by Artemis, the goddess of the hunt and Apollo's sister. Artemis, who was very attracted to Orion, actually fired her arrow in an attempt to kill the scorpion that was molesting him. Being a magnificent shot, she struck the black head that she saw bobbing in the water with her first arrow.

The goddess Artemis
This gold plaque, dating from the 7th century B.C., shows Artemis in her role as goddess of the animals.

Tragically, however, her target turned out to be Orion's head, rather than the scorpion, and the hunter was killed.

According to this latter version of the story, the grief-stricken Artemis then placed Orion as a constellation among the stars, along with his faithful dog, Syrius, where he is eternally pursued by the giant scorpion. The constellation of Orion, incidentally, sets in the sky just as the constellation of Scorpio rises.

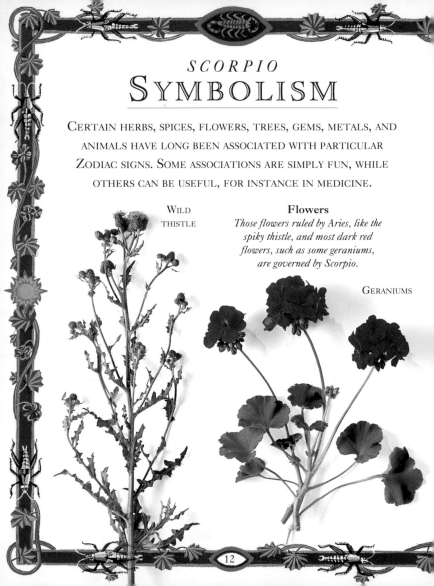

SCORPIO
SYMBOLISM

CERTAIN HERBS, SPICES, FLOWERS, TREES, GEMS, METALS, AND
ANIMALS HAVE LONG BEEN ASSOCIATED WITH PARTICULAR
ZODIAC SIGNS. SOME ASSOCIATIONS ARE SIMPLY FUN, WHILE
OTHERS CAN BE USEFUL, FOR INSTANCE IN MEDICINE.

WILD
THISTLE

Flowers
*Those flowers ruled by Aries, like the
spiky thistle, and most dark red
flowers, such as some geraniums,
are governed by Scorpio.*

GERANIUMS

Trees

The blackthorn has always been associated with Scorpio, but so are all bushy trees, such as the hawthorn, and trees that are used for hedging, like the macrocarpa.

HAWTHORN

Spices

No spices are specifically linked with Scorpio, but red or hot spices such as cayenne pepper, paprika, and chilli are sometimes associated with the sign.

PAPRIKA

Herbs

Scorpio rules the same herbs as Aries, such as peppermint. It is most strongly associated with herbs that have very dark red flowers. These include figwort, which quells itching, and dovesfoot, which is good for colic and for expelling kidney stones.

PEPPERMINT

CHILLI

SCORPIO
SYMBOLISM

RAW IRON

SCORPION

CUT STEEL
BROOCH

STEEL DOUBLE-
AXE BROOCH

JAMESI SCARAB

WEST AFRICAN
SCARAB

STEEL BRACELET

Metal
*The Scorpio metal is
traditionally said to be
either steel or iron.*

AMBER JEWELLERY

14

Animals

Ancient astrologers claimed that domestic farm animals were ruled by Scorpio. The creature of the sign is also often mentioned, and modern astrologers name all crustaceans and many insects.

JEWEL BEETLE

AMAZON SCARAB

WEST AFRICAN SCARAB

JEWEL BEETLE

SAGRA BEETLE

CENTRAL AMERICAN SCARAB

JAMESI SCARAB

Gems

Amber and the mysterious opal are the Scorpio gemstones. Opals that show changing colours have a particularly strong link with the sign.

SCORPIO
PROFILE

THE INTENSITY OF THE SCORPIO PERSONALITY IS USUALLY VISIBLE
IN THE INDIVIDUAL'S APPEARANCE AND EXPRESSION.
SHARP-EYED SCORPIOS DO NOT MISS A THING, AND ARE THE
NATURAL DETECTIVES OF THE ZODIAC.

Your determination is usually evident in your stance. You stand with your head jutting forward in a sleuth-like manner, as though you are peering through some fascinating keyhole.

The body

There are two distinct Scorpio body types. The first is heavy, giving the impression of a certain world-weariness, as if the individual has been around for a long time, and enjoyed every minute of it. The other is very lean and wiry, probably as a result of slogging it out in a health club, and burning up all that Scorpio energy. In general, Scorpios are rarely above medium height, and some can be rather short. Female Scorpios can

The Scorpio face
An obvious characteristic of the Scorpio face is an intent and piercing gaze.

become very buxom if they gain weight, but they rarely lose their figures or become any less active. They tend to swing their hips as they walk.

The face

A typical Scorpio has a fairly large forehead, and deep-set, piercing eyes. Comparisons are often drawn with the eagle, a bird that is connected with this sign. The chin is usually well formed, unless the individual is overweight, and the mouth is often extremely sensual and full lipped. A typical Scorpio will have somewhat large ears, high cheek bones, a full neck, and a wide, strong jaw. Many Scorpios have strong, but often rather coarse hair.

The Scorpio appearance

You probably possess a determined stance, and favour quite dramatic clothes in rich satins and silks.

Style

Leather and the colour black are popular among Scorpios, even when they are not particularly fashionable. You will probably favour an image that enhances sexiness, and if this is not overdone it works well. Many Scorpios like wearing tight jeans, leather trousers, and severely plunging necklines; not everyone is suited to each of these.

The texture of your clothing may be very important to you. Scorpios usually like the smoothness of satin and pure silk. Velvet is also popular. Any sharp, or remotely coarse material, such as wool, will probably hold no appeal for you.

On formal occasions Scorpios usually look extremely smart in somewhat severe clothes. You will not submerge your personality by dressing conventionally. All that has to be done is for you to study how to make fashion work for you. You will instinctively want to exploit your own personal image as far as you possibly can, and there is no reason why you should not do so.

In general

Many Zodiac types consciously or unconsciously tend to aspire to the image of their sign, and in Scorpios this can be very much the case. This can be amusing, but it may also be overdone. Scorpios like a sense of mystery, and in extreme cases the women can be *femmes fatales*. If you try and maintain a sense of humour, all will be well.

PERSONALITY

YOU ARE LIKELY TO HAVE A STRIKING, INTENSE PERSONALITY, AND THE POTENTIAL TO BE A BIG ACHIEVER. IF, HOWEVER, THIS POTENTIAL IS NOT FULLY EXPRESSED, YOU CAN BECOME NEGATIVE IN OUTLOOK.

Having a strong, passionate belief in whatever you do will lead to a full expression of the remarkable resources of both physical and emotional energy that you possess, which are characteristic of all Scorpios.

At work

It must be said that Scorpios with no clear objective in life, who are uninvolved in their work or in any other activity worthwhile for them, can be difficult, uncooperative, stubborn, and impervious to reason. In all, they will be a thorough pain to the people around them.

It is worth remembering that while Pluto, Scorpio's ruling planet, can enable its subjects to overcome obstacles, it can also encourage a host of negative tendencies, for instance slyness, cruelty, and an urge to be somewhat overly critical. These negative characteristics, which can sometimes constitute a fairly considerable force, may make Scorpios illogically jealous of other people's achievements; especially their partner's. It may even come to the point where they will start to act in an underhand and vindictive fashion, and scheme towards their rivals' downfall, giving way to outbursts of unpleasant, illogical rage when others offer help or advice.

Your attitudes

When all is well with you, however, you will know exactly what it is that you want to do in life, and will certainly see to it that whatever this is gets done. When it is properly fulfilled, this powerful and demanding motivation will lead to your finding that vital sense of inner satisfaction upon which so much of life can rest. The urge to move ambitiously forward will then follow from it, encouraging you to better and greater achievements. You will no

Pluto rules Scorpio

*Pluto, god of the underworld, represents the ruling planet of Scorpio.
The influence of Pluto can encourage its subjects to overcome obstacles,
but may also make them critical, cruel, and secretive.*

doubt value your friends highly, and are likely to strive very hard in order to make your relationships work.

The overall picture
Scorpios tend to fling themselves straight into projects, whether these involve starting a business venture or embarking on demanding intellectual study. You will probably work very hard on any project for some time, and achieve many of the goals that you set yourself. Then, for no apparent reason, you will throw up the whole venture and start again from the bottom of another hill.

Having said all of this, for the most part, Scorpios enjoy life, living it to the full and encouraging their friends and loved ones to do the same.

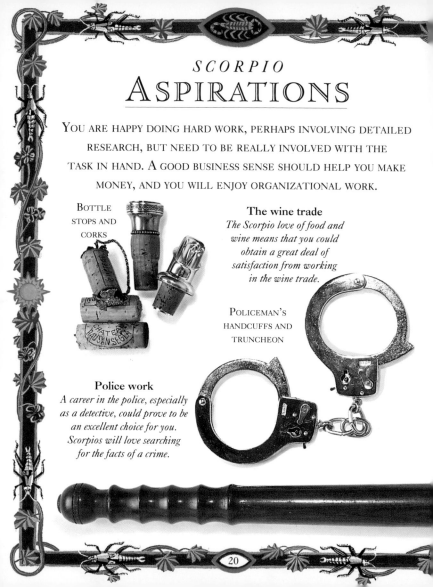

SCORPIO
ASPIRATIONS

YOU ARE HAPPY DOING HARD WORK, PERHAPS INVOLVING DETAILED
RESEARCH, BUT NEED TO BE REALLY INVOLVED WITH THE
TASK IN HAND. A GOOD BUSINESS SENSE SHOULD HELP YOU MAKE
MONEY, AND YOU WILL ENJOY ORGANIZATIONAL WORK.

BOTTLE
STOPS AND
CORKS

The wine trade
*The Scorpio love of food and
wine means that you could
obtain a great deal of
satisfaction from working
in the wine trade.*

POLICEMAN'S
HANDCUFFS AND
TRUNCHEON

Police work
*A career in the police, especially
as a detective, could prove to be
an excellent choice for you.
Scorpios will love searching
for the facts of a crime.*

1930s MINING AND
ENGINEERING
CIGARETTE
CARDS

RIFLE BULLETS

Mining and engineering
*Many Scorpios enjoy examining the
Earth's resources. An interest in ecology
often persuades them to discover positive
ways of exploiting them.*

The armed forces
*Scorpio is a water sign, and many of its
subjects join the navy. The army may,
however, also prove attractive. Many
famous generals share a
Scorpio Sun sign.*

CLAY PIGGY
BANK
AND BANK
NOTES

Banking
*A fascination for making
money and seeing it grow
can lead to careers
in banking and the
stock exchange.*

SCORPIO
HEALTH

THE SCORPIO BODY AREA IS THE GENITALS, AND IT IS THIS
RELATIONSHIP THAT HAS GIVEN THE SIGN ITS OFTEN
UNJUSTIFIED REPUTATION FOR OVERT SEXINESS. MANY OTHER
FACTORS SHAPE THE SCORPIO CHARACTER.

Scorpio can, in a number of ways,
be considered the most powerful
sign of the Zodiac. Its subjects are
often fortunate enough to possess
tremendous resources of both physical
and emotional energy. In order for
you to be both psychologically whole
and in the best physical shape, you
must be prepared to shape your life in
such a way that both of these areas
manage to find some
form of positive
expression.

Your diet
For most Scorpios, food is something
that has to be enjoyed. You may, for
instance, like a lot of rich food and
wine, and dieting could prove to be
difficult. You might benefit from
supplementing your diet with the cell
salt Kali Muriaticum (Kali. Mur.).

Taking care
When lacking any real objective in
life, or suffering from a lack of
physical exercise, a Sun sign Scorpio
will become discontented, depressed,
and unwell. Brooding on the situation
is only likely to make matters
worse. All Scorpios must realize
that they need demanding
projects in life, of both an
intellectual and physical
nature. You require goals
towards which you can aim
and direct your abundance
of energy, and if all is well
you will achieve them.

Tomatoes
*The foods ruled by Aries, like
tomatoes, are also associated
with Scorpio.*

Astrology and the body

For many centuries it was impossible to practice medicine without a knowledge of astrology. In European universities, medical training included information on how planetary positions would affect the administration of medicines, the bleeding of patients, and the right time to pick herbs and make potions. Each Zodiac sign rules a particular part of the body, and early medical textbooks always included a drawing that illustrated the point.

SCORPIO AT
LEISURE

EACH OF THE SUN SIGNS TRADITIONALLY SUGGESTS SPARE-TIME
ACTIVITIES, HOBBIES, AND HOLIDAY DESTINATIONS.
ALTHOUGH THESE ARE ONLY SUGGESTIONS, THEY OFTEN WORK
OUT WELL, AND ARE WORTH TESTING.

POSTAGE STAMPS

Motor racing
*The speed and great risk
involved in fast motor-
cycling and driving can
prove compulsive for
many Scorpios.*

Travel
*You will enjoy visiting exotic
locations such as Morocco,
Syria, and Uruguay. Bavaria
and Norway may also appeal.*

1930S CYCLE AND
MOTOR RACING CARDS

TROUT-FISHING FLY

1920S MAGNIFYING GLASS

Fishing
*Water sign Scorpios often
love sitting on a river bank
with a fishing rod.*

Detective fiction
*With their inquiring minds,
Scorpios will enjoy unravelling
the plot of a good detective novel.*

Sailing
*The fact that Scorpio is a water
sign could mean that you are
drawn to all kinds of aquatic
sports, including sailing.*

SAILOR'S KNOT

HOTEL BELL

Hotel holidays
*Scorpios enjoy life, so the luxury
and comfort of expensive hotels
with excellent facilities may
well appeal to you.*

Beach holidays
*A beach holiday will afford
you the opportunity for
water sports, such as
scuba diving, which
are usually enjoyed
by Scorpios.*

RED ROSE

SEA SHELLS AND SAND

Seduction
*Scorpios take their
love and sex lives
very seriously, but
there is no doubt
that seduction can
become a hobby for
some of you.*

SCORPIO IN
LOVE

THE PASSIONATE EMOTION OF SCORPIO IS AT ITS MOST POTENT IN
LOVE AND IN SEXUAL RELATIONSHIPS. THE NEED FOR SEXUAL
FULFILMENT IS IMPORTANT FOR THIS ZODIAC TYPE, BUT MANY
ASTROLOGICAL WRITERS TEND TO OVERSTATE IT.

You may find it difficult to unburden yourself by talking things through with a sympathetic friend, let alone your partner. Therapy may provide a solution.

Scorpios have a great capacity for true love, and are therefore able to contribute much to the success of a long-term relationship. The worst

Scorpio fault is jealousy, and if you find yourself acting jealously towards your partner, it can really spoil your happiness. Being aware of this tendency can help to counter it.

As a lover
Despite the traditional emphasis on Scorpio sexuality, it is wrong to think that all members of this sign are always on the rampage, moving from one conquest to the next.

Much of a Scorpio's abundant resources of emotional and physical energy are oriented towards their sex life. However, once you have found a responsive mate, with an equal level of need, fulfilment is not hard to find. Your sexual needs will take their place in a balanced life.

Types of Scorpio lover
Scorpios are capable of expressing love and sex in one of at least five different ways. One group

takes a somewhat clinical view of love, in extreme cases suspecting that there is something "dirty" about sex. People in this group are very discriminating, can be critical, and must be helped to relax if their inhibition is not to spoil things. A second group is romantic, with a liking for glamorous settings. Members of this group usually enjoy a slow build-up to love-making, and are probably eager to enter into a permanent relationship, but may be indecisive about commitment. Another group consists of those people who may be called "pure Scorpios". They are generally capable of loving someone both deeply and passionately, but must guard against jealousy and emotional outbursts. A fourth group is lively and enthusiastic about

sex, but may sometimes take their relationships rather less seriously than other Scorpios. Finally, there are those members of this Sun sign group who are somewhat cooler in their emotional responses than the other Scorpios. These people are normally very faithful within a relationship once they have decided to commit themselves firmly to a partner. They often end up sharing their life with a person who is much wealthier than they are.

SCORPIO ROOMS CAN BE ALMOST TOO COMFORTABLE. THEY MAY HAVE A SEDUCTIVE AIR, WHICH WILL BE ACHIEVED THROUGH DARK COLOURS AND SUBDUED LIGHTING. THIS CHARACTERISTIC COULD APPLY TO ALL THE ROOMS IN YOUR HOME.

Your ideal home would be placed on the edge of an idyllic lake. However, you will probably have to compromise over this, so some form of water garden, or perhaps a well, might provide a pleasant alternative. You are also likely to feel very much at home in the city.

Furniture

There is a certain slickness in the furniture Scorpios choose and, most often, it will be covered in leather; black is popular. Comfort is important, so while settees may be bold in appearance, they will actually be soft and seductive. You will spend a great deal of money on furnishings, and are unlikely to take risks when choosing items that will have to be lived with for a long period of time. A classic Barcelona chair is very popular, combining as it does style, tradition, and a smart, expensive elegance. Scorpios are very image conscious in their choice of furniture as well as their clothes.

Soft furnishings

The Scorpio colour is basically deep crimson, which is the colour of Pluto, the Scorpio ruling planet, and the overall effect of your furnishings may be rather dark. It will, however, be very rich, and there will be no lack of cushions to enhance comfort. These will often match the upholstery itself or be printed in an exotic pattern such as paisley. Dark shades of heavy satin

Stuffed alligator

An article such as this will enhance the overall air of mystery that many Scorpios are attracted to.

can be popular, because texture is often important for Scorpios. Rugs will have a heavy pile, and curtains will be well lined and contribute to a somewhat seductive atmosphere.

Decorative objects

A visitor's eye will be drawn very quickly to the decorative objects that you choose. They will be very striking and will make definite statements. Your choice of paintings will be dramatic and colourful; Gauguin is often a popular choice because of his sensual colours and subject matter. You may also like surreal and imaginative paintings, or energetic and aggressive works. Young Scorpios could favour posters of hard rock

Wine and grapes
The richness of dark red grapes and wine boldly reflects the intensely seductive Scorpio image.

groups. A bowl of luscious fruit, and perhaps some splendid wine, may also be in evidence – they will blend beautifully with the appearance of the overall scheme. Something in metal, such as a pot or an antique weapon, could also be present, or perhaps some decorative coloured glass.

The lighting arrangement in your home is probably rather subdued. This is in keeping with the need for privacy that many Scorpios have. A well-positioned spotlight may be used to enhance the appearance of one of your favourite objects, such as a vase, an unusual antique, or a painting that you find particularly attractive.

Barcelona chair
Combining style, tradition, and expensive elegance with the texture of leather, this chair is a clear choice for the Scorpio home.

THE
MOON
AND
YOU

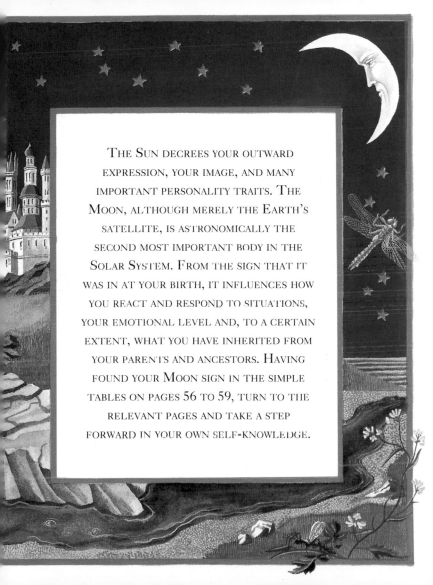

THE SUN DECREES YOUR OUTWARD
EXPRESSION, YOUR IMAGE, AND MANY
IMPORTANT PERSONALITY TRAITS. THE
MOON, ALTHOUGH MERELY THE EARTH'S
SATELLITE, IS ASTRONOMICALLY THE
SECOND MOST IMPORTANT BODY IN THE
SOLAR SYSTEM. FROM THE SIGN THAT IT
WAS IN AT YOUR BIRTH, IT INFLUENCES HOW
YOU REACT AND RESPOND TO SITUATIONS,
YOUR EMOTIONAL LEVEL AND, TO A CERTAIN
EXTENT, WHAT YOU HAVE INHERITED FROM
YOUR PARENTS AND ANCESTORS. HAVING
FOUND YOUR MOON SIGN IN THE SIMPLE
TABLES ON PAGES 56 TO 59, TURN TO THE
RELEVANT PAGES AND TAKE A STEP
FORWARD IN YOUR OWN SELF-KNOWLEDGE.

THE MOON IN
ARIES

THE FIERY EMOTIONAL ENERGY OF YOUR ARIEN MOON IS BACKED
UP BY THE INTENSE ENERGY OF SCORPIO. YOU NEED
BOTH PHYSICAL AND PSYCHOLOGICAL FULFILMENT IN LIFE, AND
SHOULD NEVER ALLOW YOURSELF TO STAGNATE.

Scorpio and Aries are both very powerful Zodiac signs, bestowing on their subjects a high level of emotional and physical energy. Your Scorpio intensity is heightened by your Arien sense of immediacy and instinct to be first.

Self-expression
With this Sun and Moon combination you will not be prepared to allow opponents to get the better of you. Inner fulfilment is essential to you, and your way of achieving it is to fill every day with work. Avoid time-filling jobs, or a career in which you have no real interest but pursue solely for money. If you have a job that is dull, make sure that your leisure hours are challenging and lively.

Romance
You have a high emotional level, and are very passionate. This passion will find its best expression within your

relationships. You will possess rather less of a smouldering intensity than many Sun sign Scorpios, and will approach love and sex with an uncomplicated enthusiasm.

The worst Arien fault is selfishness. If anyone accuses you of this, listen to them, as they will probably be right.

Due to a tendency to act rather prematurely, you may feel inclined to deepen an emotional relationship too early. When this appears likely to happen, allow the critical faculties of your Scorpio Sun extra expression.

Your well-being
The Arien body area is the head, and you may therefore suffer from headaches, perhaps because of the way other people are acting. On the other hand, they may sometimes stem from slight kidney upsets. Because Aries promotes hastiness, you might be rather accident-prone and could regularly incur minor cuts and bruises.

The Moon in Aries

Planning ahead

Your Scorpio business sense is spiced with the Arien spirit of enterprise. Should you start a business venture, you will find this not only enjoyable, but also probably very financially rewarding. You are shrewd and capable with money, but may need to consciously think twice before investing, since you could be a little too enthusiastic about schemes that seem solid, but may in fact be hollow. If you give yourself time to think, your Scorpio shrewdness will come into its own and you will manage to avoid coming to grief.

Parenthood

You will make an energetic and lively parent, and will expect a lot from your children. You will discipline them in a positive way, and will not find it difficult to keep well up with all of their concerns and opinions. This should avoid any problems with the generation gap.

THE MOON IN
TAURUS

SCORPIO AND TAURUS ARE POLAR ZODIAC SIGNS, SO YOU WERE BORN
UNDER A FULL MOON. AVOID RESTLESSNESS
BY ALLOWING YOUR PRACTICAL MOON SIGN TO STEADY YOUR
POWERFUL EMOTIONS, AND CONTROL JEALOUSY.

Everyone, in one way or another, expresses elements of their polar or opposite sign (the sign that lies across the Zodiac circle from their Sun sign). For Scorpios, this is Taurus and, as the Moon was in that sign when you were born, this polarity is emphasized in an interesting way.

Self-expression
The Moon is, traditionally, "well placed" in Taurus. This means that its psychological effect on you is somewhat above average.

In order for you to develop your full potential and live life in a satisfying and rewarding way, you need great emotional and financial security. When you have it, you flourish, and are capable of great achievements. Without it, your lifestyle suffers.

Even more than many Sun sign Scorpios, you must always have an objective in view, and should carve your way towards it constructively.

Romance
Both Scorpio and Taurus are of the fixed quality and, as a result, you can be rather stubborn. Taurus, like Scorpio, is a passionate sign. It will therefore increase the smouldering intensity that your Sun sign gives you.

You will express your feelings in a warm and affectionate way, and are capable of giving great sexual enjoyment. However, the worst Taurean fault is possessiveness and, if this is ignited by Scorpio jealousy, you could well have problems. Be aware that these negative emotions could spoil your relationships.

Your need for emotional security could cause you to create something of a claustrophobic atmosphere, which some partners might resent.

Your well-being
The Taurean body area covers the neck and throat. Colds will almost certainly settle in that area, so take

The Moon in Taurus

care of it, especially in winter. Taurus likes good food, and so does Scorpio. Living it up can therefore mean considerable weight gain, unless you have a high metabolic rate. Moderation and exercise will help.

Planning ahead

You will be clever with money, and have a great instinct for investment. Therefore your bank balance and portfolio of shares, however small, will grow to your satisfaction. However, you certainly love luxury and will therefore also spend freely. You will probably be able to cope with your finances without professional advice.

Parenthood

You are conventional and may be somewhat conservative in outlook. Be careful: your children could accuse you of being old-fashioned. You will work hard for them, but might be stricter than you realize. If you try to keep up with all their concerns, you should have few problems with the generation gap.

THE MOON IN
GEMINI

YOU ARE MORE LOGICAL AND LESS INTUITIVE THAN MANY
SCORPIOS. IT IS PROBABLE THAT YOU CAN USEFULLY
RATIONALIZE YOUR EMOTIONS AND INTELLECTUALIZE ANY
DEEP-ROOTED PSYCHOLOGICAL PROBLEMS OR WORRIES.

The combination of two very different signs makes for a dynamic influence on your character. Gemini is an air sign, and is intellectually oriented; it therefore adds a lightness and inquisitiveness to your Scorpio Sun, which is intensive and really needs to get to the root of every problem.

Self-expression
When challenged in any way, you will at once respond with lively, searching questions. You will be very sceptical of every theory put to you.

It may be that you are attracted to the media, and all kinds of research could well fascinate you. You are an excellent communicator, and this can be of advantage not only in your career, but also on a personal level.

When moved, you will probably try to rationalize your emotions. By all means go in for self-analysis, but remember that in the process you can rationalize away a lot of pleasure. Like many Sun sign Scorpios, you may tend to bottle up your problems. However, you should not suffer badly from this tendency, due to the communicative nature of your Geminian Moon.

Romance
In addition to expressing Scorpio passion and achieving sexual fulfilment, you also find it very rewarding to enjoy a high level of intellectual rapport and friendship within an emotional relationship.

It is particularly good for you to have a partner who is at least your intellectual equal, if not considerably up ahead of you.

Your well-being
Scorpios tend to be whole-hoggers, liking a lot of everything. If you smoke, you will probably smoke heavily, and this is inadvisable given

The Moon in Gemini

that the Gemini organ is the lungs. You have quite a high level of nervous energy, and should aim to burn up both it and your Scorpio physical energy positively, in sport or perhaps through fast, demanding exercise.

Planning ahead

You may be somewhat less skilful with money than many Sun sign Scorpios. You have a natural selling ability, and are capable of organizing profitable deals. Are you, however, perhaps a little too easily attracted to get-rich-quick schemes that, in the long run, turn into get-poor-quickly disasters? When tempted, remember to make thorough enquiries.

Parenthood

You probably find it easy to keep up with your children, and enjoy discussing their opinions. At times, you could even be ahead of them, and may surprise them with your knowledge of current trends. You should have few problems with the generation gap.

THE MOON IN
CANCER

YOUR CANCERIAN MOON INCREASES YOUR SENSITIVE AWARENESS
OF OTHERS' NEEDS. YOU HAVE A PROTECTIVE INSTINCT,
AND GREAT EMOTIONAL ENERGY. CHANNEL THESE POSITIVELY,
AND BEWARE OF IRRATIONAL WORRY.

Because Scorpio and Cancer are both water signs, the level of your emotional energy is very high. You should always be sure that you have positive and demanding ways of expressing it. You are a power-house of strong feeling and, for your psychological comfort, must be intensely involved in work that you find totally rewarding.

Self-expression

Your Cancerian Moon is likely to make you very intuitive, and you have an active imagination that you should make every effort to express creatively. If this does not happen, you will worry irrationally, and could spend too much time waiting for the worst to happen. Try to also recognize the fact that, perhaps as the result of your sensitivity to atmospheres and other people's reactions, you may sometimes be prone to bouts of moodiness. Aim to keep your outlook positive, and endeavour to be more optimistic than you may naturally be inclined to feel.

Romance

You are a wonderfully sensual and highly sexed lover, good at assessing your partner's needs. You are also demanding, and need a partner who is not only active but also sympathetic. Watch out, though, for a tendency to "mother" your partners. This can create a rather claustrophobic atmosphere, which more freedom-loving partners may resent.

Your well-being

The Cancerian body area covers the breasts and chest. While there is absolutely no connection between this sign and the disease that bears the same name, Cancerian women should be as diligent as all their sisters in regularly examining their breasts. To some extent the digestive system

The Moon in Cancer

is also Cancer-ruled and, when you are worried, you could find your stomach giving you trouble. Cancerians and Scorpios enjoy their food, which will not help. You may need to take quite tough exercise to keep flab at bay.

Planning ahead

There is a fair chance that you could be something of a financial wizard. You possess Cancerian shrewdness, with the additional business acumen that springs from your Scorpio Sun. This gives you the capacity to make a lot of money, provided that you do

not give in to the Scorpio tendency to suddenly stop what you are doing and begin a new project.

Parenthood

You will enjoy the responsibilities of family life, and may well be very keen to have your own home and children.

You will be pretty strict with your children, which is fine. Do, however, allow them the freedom to express themselves. Avoid being sentimental, and harking back to the past, when you were a child. If you get involved in your children's interests, you will bridge the generation gap.

THE MOON IN
LEO

YOU ARE A WHOLE-HOGGER, AND YOUR SCORPIO INTENSITY AND
ENERGY ARE SPICED WITH A POWERFUL CREATIVE INSTINCT
THAT YOU SHOULD EXPRESS AS FREELY AS YOU CAN. BE AWARE,
HOWEVER, THAT YOU ARE PRONE TO STUBBORNNESS.

Your Scorpio personality is exaggerated by the fiery emotion and energy of your Leo Moon. You have a great deal of inner strength and determination, and marvellous organizational ability. However, you should be very careful not to become autocratic and domineering.

Self-expression
Your Scorpio passion and powerful motivation are enhanced by your instinct to do your very best, and to develop every hobby and interest, as well as your career, to the highest standard. The result is that you are probably very good at everything you do. You are one of the world's workers, and will fill every day with useful activity.

Both Scorpio and Leo are signs that are highly charged with emotion, and Leo emotion is warm, fiery, and enthusiastic. It will make you look at life in a positive, optimistic way.

Romance
Your lovemaking has style, elegance, and more than a hint of glamour, and you will see to it that your partners enjoy life as much as you do, both in and out of bed.

Both Scorpio and Leo are of the fixed quality, which means that you can be very stubborn at times. Make an effort to reassess your opinions from time to time, and never mind admitting your mistakes.

The worst Leo fault is bossiness, so be careful that this unpleasant trait does not mar your relationships.

Your well-being
The Leo body area is the spine and back, so you need exercise to keep these in good working order. A backrest chair is also an excellent idea if you work for long hours at a desk.

The Leo organ is the heart, and this needs regular exercise. You may find exercise rather boring, so aim to

The Moon in Leo

join a good health club, or perhaps dance or movement classes, where some of your dramatic qualities can find creative expression.

Scorpio and Leo could encourage you to have a rather rich diet. Try to keep this in check, otherwise you may well put on weight.

Planning ahead

You need to earn a lot of money to cater for what are probably expensive tastes. Your financial flair and potential for success should, however, enable you to do this. You will enjoy keeping an eye on your bank

statements and seeing your money grow, and will usually invest wisely, but resist any tendency to put too many financial eggs in one basket.

Parenthood

You will enjoy your children, but could sometimes seem rather pompous to them, and perhaps conventional. Try to see life through their eyes, and you will avoid problems with the generation gap. If you use your lively, enthusiastic Moon qualities, and are encouraging rather than critical, you will certainly win your children's love and respect.

THE MOON IN
VIRGO

YOUR VIRGOAN MOON WILL ENSURE THAT YOU WILL NOT BE
SATISFIED UNTIL YOU HAVE GOT TO THE ROOT OF EVERY
PROBLEM. BE CAREFUL, SINCE YOU COULD BECOME OBSESSIVE,
AND TRY NOT TO GET TOO BOGGED DOWN IN DETAIL.

Your water sign Sun and earth sign Moon combine well, and share several complementary characteristics. Scorpio enjoys mystery, and getting to the roots of problems; your Virgoan Moon will encourage you to analyze them.

Self-expression
You are among the natural sleuths of the Zodiac, and will therefore enjoy any kind of research. Be careful, however, that in examining the minutiae of a problem you do not miss seeing the overall pattern, and try to develop breadth of vision.

You have a great deal of common sense, and a very practical approach to life. However, you must keep a tendency to worry under control.

Romance
The influence of Virgo is unlikely to be highly charged, emotionally. Some of your Scorpio passion will therefore be moderated by your Moon sign. You will work hard to make your relationships work, possibly rather gradually overcoming any Virgoan timidity in your response to sex. As your tension eases and your Scorpio Sun takes over, you will find yourself enjoying an ever-increasing richness in this sphere of your life.

Your well-being
The Virgoan organ is the stomach, and you may suffer from stomach disorders when you are worried. You need a high-fibre diet.

A Virgoan influence brings with it a great deal of nervous energy. This can sometimes lead to a build-up of stress and tension, which may result in migraine. Try to relax. Outdoor exercise may help you, and so will talking things over with a friend. A relaxation technique such as yoga may prove to be useful, as will walking, cycling, and jogging.

The Moon in Virgo

Planning ahead

You may be rather less of a big spender than many Scorpios, and will probably be good at balancing the books. There is even a chance that you could feel slightly guilty whenever you are extravagant. Do your best to ensure that you do not, and enjoy yourself. In particular, make sure that you do not hesitate when it comes to spending money on a favourite hobby, and splash out on good fabric, materials, tools, and machines. If you are at all apprehensive about how to invest your money, take financial advice.

Parenthood

Be careful not to be too critical of your children's efforts. You could deflate them far more than you realize.

Scorpios are usually fairly strict, but always retain the capacity for fun. If you listen to your children's opinions, you will encounter very few problems with the generation gap.

THE MOON IN
LIBRA

YOU SOMETIMES APPEAR A LITTLE LAZY BECAUSE YOUR
LIBRAN MOON ENCOURAGES YOU TO RELAX AND STUDY
EVERY ASPECT OF A PROBLEM. YOU ARE MORE CONSIDERATE
OF OTHER PEOPLE THAN MANY SUN SIGN SCORPIOS.

The charm of your Libran Moon softens the powerful intensity of your Scorpio personality, and you always respond warmly and sympathetically to other people.

Self-expression
It may be that you are rather slower to come to decisions than many Scorpios, because your immediate reaction is to hesitate; you usually want to think at least twice before committing yourself.

You are tactful and diplomatic, especially when put on the spot in a difficult situation, and can produce the right answer at the right time. The influence of your Libran Moon will encourage you to always have time for other people.

Romance
You are among the more romantic of Scorpios, and enjoy the relaxed development of a relationship almost as much as a passionate scene. You will be considerate of your partners, and will understand their needs.

A serious Libran fault is resentment, and you must guard against a tendency to cling to past differences or minor misdemeanours that your partner may have made.

Your well-being
The Libran body area is the lumbar region of the back. If you are prone to back pain, consider purchasing a backrest chair. The Libran organ is the kidneys and, as the result of a slight imbalance in that area, you may suffer from headaches.

Unless you are a quick-moving, wiry Scorpio type, your Moon sign may give you a rather slow metabolism. This can mean that with a Libran emphasis on good, rich, and sometimes sweet food, you may put on weight too easily. Vigorous exercise will help, but you will

The Moon in Libra

probably find that physical activity will need to be accompanied by another, perhaps philosophical, element. Yoga, tai chi, and tantra are worth considering.

Planning ahead

You are more generous than the average person, and the immediate attraction of expensive clothes or fine items for the home may prove so tempting that your excellent Scorpio financial good sense could suffer. It might be advisable for you to take

professional advice when investing. Regular, steadily growing savings schemes are good for you.

Parenthood

You will alternate between being a strict parent and a bit of a soft touch. Make certain that your children know where they stand with you, and you will develop an affectionate rapport. If you keep up with their ideas, and always try to be aware of their problems, you will avoid difficulties with the generation gap.

THE MOON IN
SCORPIO

WITH BOTH THE SUN AND THE MOON IN SCORPIO ON THE DAY
OF YOUR BIRTH, YOU WERE BORN UNDER A NEW MOON.
SINCE SCORPIO IS A WATER SIGN, THIS ELEMENT IS IMPORTANT,
AND YOU WILL HAVE MANY SCORPIO CHARACTERISTICS.

Should you read a list of the characteristics of your Scorpio Sun sign, you will probably realize that a great many of them apply to you. On average, out of a list of, say, 20 personality traits of any particular Sun sign, most people will identify with 11 or 12. However, because the Moon was also in Scorpio when you were born, for you the average increases considerably.

Self-expression
You will react to most situations with a keen incisiveness, getting to the root of a matter and thrashing out every detail in the most searching way.

It is essential for all Scorpios to be emotionally involved in their work, but for you this is even more the case.

Romance
You are highly sexed and very passionate, and it is as important for you to share a rewarding relationship with someone as it is to have a satisfying job. You will contribute a great deal towards the success of your relationship, but must be aware that you are a very demanding partner. You need to share your life with someone who both realizes and understands this.

You would also do well to remember that you can sometimes be extremely susceptible to jealousy, and that this tendency can often cause problems between you and your lover.

Your well-being
As far as your health is concerned, you stand a fair chance of being particularly vulnerable to Scorpio ailments (*see pages 22 – 23*). Bear in mind that Sun sign Scorpios are whole-hoggers, and that this applies to you more than to most people of your Sun sign. Try to keep your food intake in balance, and aim for a certain amount of moderation.

The Moon in Scorpio

You will probablty enjoy all kinds of winter sport, and perhaps heavy team games. It is more than likely that you will want to become very involved in whatever sport you decide to take up, and that you will be capable of great dedication to it.

Planning ahead

You should have considerable financial flair, and plenty of intuition when it comes to investment. You may find a career in big business or banking rewarding. Be careful to spread your investments – while you are very capable of making a lot of money, do not over-invest.

Parenthood

You will be very keen for your children to make good progress, and may consequently tend to push them a little too hard, and be rather strict with them. Make a conscious effort to be sympathetic towards their ideas and problems.

THE MOON IN
SAGITTARIUS

YOUR SAGITTARIAN MOON MODERATES THE INTENSE SIDE OF
YOUR PERSONALITY. YOU CAN GRASP AN OVERALL
SITUATION FAR MORE EASILY THAN MOST SCORPIOS, AND
ARE NOT AS OBSESSED WITH DETAIL.

The qualities attributed to Scorpio and Sagittarius are very different. As a result you have some contrasting facets to your personality. You possess natural optimism and enthusiasm, which surfaces as soon as a project is put to you, or whenever you meet with a challenge.

Self-expression
Many Scorpios are properly described as "deep". Such a description is less applicable to you, and you do not find it difficult to be open and frank.

Your capacity to enjoy life, especially when you are confronted by challenge, is wonderful. You will hate the thought of wasting time even more than others of your Sun sign.

Romance
As well as burning Scorpio passion, you have a fiery liveliness in your expression of love and sex. You will probably enjoy many relationships

during the course of your life and, once you are committed to a partner, you will still need a certain amount of freedom of expression.

Be careful that Scorpio jealousy does not complicate your life. Despite your instinct for independence, you will not be very happy if your partner shows signs of being even mildly flirtatious. Remember that you are capable of similar behaviour, and relent a little.

Your well-being
Scorpios usually love rich and often expensive food. Sagittarians are not averse to it, either, and also love good wines and beers. The Sagittarian organ is the liver, so that in your case excesses of wining and dining may easily lead to liverishness.

The Sagittarian body area covers the hips and thighs, and women with this sign emphasized have a tendency to put on weight in that area.

The Moon in Sagittarius

Moderation does not come naturally to either Scorpio or Sagittarius; both types find it very boring. Self-discipline is therefore important. On the credit side, Sagittarians usually like energetic exercise, so you should not find it too difficult to get involved in an appealing exercise regime.

Planning ahead

Although you will, no doubt, have the Scorpio ability to make money, you may enjoy gambling, and could find risky financial schemes attractive. Be careful, since you could lose a lot of hard-earned money in this way.

You may do well as an investor, as long as you do not take undue risks. Be aware of the extremes to which you may succumb, and maintain a balanced outlook.

Parenthood

You will be among the most lively and positive of Scorpio parents. You have the ability to share a lot of fun with your children, and will encourage them in their efforts, both intellectual and physical. You will not find it too hard to understand your children's problems, and the generation gap should hold no terrors for you.

THE MOON IN
CAPRICORN

YOUR OBJECTIVES ARE IMPORTANT TO YOU, AND YOU WILL SEIZE
EVERY OPPORTUNITY TO ACHIEVE YOUR GOALS. DO NOT
MISS OUT ON THE LIGHTER SIDE OF LIFE OR ALLOW YOUR
AMBITION TO INTERFERE WITH YOUR RELATIONSHIPS.

The water element of your Scorpio Sun and the earth element of your Capricornian Moon blend well, giving you the potential to be among the most successful of Scorpio Sun and Moon combinations.

Self-expression
You take life very seriously, but have an unusual and very off-beat sense of humour that emerges naturally and often very unexpectedly.

Your objectives and ambitions are very important to you, and you get a great deal of fulfilment from pursuing them, but you should take care that you do not miss out on enjoying life – you may veer towards becoming a workaholic. Try to avoid bringing too much work home from the office.

Romance
Your powerful Scorpio emotions are calmed by your Capricornian Moon. Your reactions to situations are logical and practical, and you are rather less likely to be emotionally moved than many Scorpios. Sometimes, you may even give the impression that you are slightly aloof.

Your approach to your love and sex life is less passionate than that of many Scorpios, and you are likely to be very faithful once committed.

Your well-being
The Capricornian body area covers the knees and shins, and yours are therefore more vulnerable than other people's. It is essential that you keep moving, because people with an emphasis on Capricorn are prone to stiffness of the joints, and rheumatic and arthritic pain.

It is unlikely that you will have a weight problem, since your Capricornian Moon has probably given you a rather lean frame, and you are possibly less attracted to heavy, rich food than is the case with many

The Moon in Capricorn

Scorpios. The teeth are also ruled by Capricorn, so be careful not to neglect to have regular dental check-ups.

Planning ahead

You are, or have the potential to be, something of a financial wizard. Capricornians are often good at business, as are Scorpios. If you are self-employed, you should be able to build up your business extremely well, provided you pace its development. The same thing applies if you have cash to invest.

Parenthood

Perhaps you need to reassess your attitude to your children, since you may be far stricter than you realize. Most children thrive when they have a secure structure to their lives, but do try to avoid damaging put-downs. Also make sure that you have time to enjoy their company as opposed to just working hard to ensure that they have all the material needs of life. Consciously tune into their opinions and concerns, otherwise you might experience generation gap problems.

THE MOON IN
AQUARIUS

STUBBORNNESS CAN BE A PROBLEM FOR YOU, BUT YOU ARE
WELL ABLE TO DETACH YOURSELF RATIONALLY FROM
DIFFICULTIES AND TO BE VERY OBJECTIVE IN ASSESSING THEM.
BE FORWARD-LOOKING, AND TRY TO KEEP AN OPEN MIND.

Your Aquarian Moon enables you to approach problems in an unusual way. Your reaction to situations is usually logical, and you can detach yourself from your emotions and see any difficulties from various angles, quickly focusing on each before reaching practical and often unique conclusions.

Self-expression
Lateral thinking comes naturally to you, and colleagues and friends often have cause to be very grateful for your originality. Because both Scorpio and Aquarius are of the fixed quality, you may be very stubborn at times. Be aware of this negative tendency, otherwise you may be accused of bloody-mindedness.

Romance
Life may not be particularly easy when you are beginning to solidify a personal relationship. You are a passionate Scorpio, but may, early on in a relationship, send out signals warning people to keep their distance.

You need sexual fulfilment as much as, or perhaps more than, anyone else. However, your independence will be important to you, and you must therefore try to find partners who will not resent this need. You may delay a long-term commitment or marriage, which is no bad thing: take your time if you feel that you should.

Your well-being
The ankles are the Aquarian body area, and yours are likely to be vulnerable, especially if you enjoy wearing some types of fashionable shoes. The circulation is also Aquarius-ruled, so take care that you look after yours. Obviously, all exercise regimes and sporting activities are a great help, and you should find time for them. Scorpios usually enjoy swimming and other

The Moon in Aquarius

water sports, but you may also be attracted to winter sports, and could be good at them.

Planning ahead

While Sun sign Scorpios are usually quite clever with money, your originality may sometimes get the better of you, and you could end up committing yourself without due thought to some exciting but not very practical scheme that catches your imagination. Financial loss will

probably follow. Aim for conventionality where finance is concerned. Express your originality and more unconventional leanings in other ways.

Parenthood

Although you will initially respond well to your children's more extreme ideas and suggestions, you may end up backtracking. Try to avoid this. Make a conscious effort to see life through their eyes.

THE MOON IN
PISCES

YOUR POWERFUL SCORPIO CHARACTERISTICS ARE SOFTENED BY THE
TENDER EMOTION OF YOUR PISCEAN MOON. YOU ARE KIND
AND MORE SENSITIVE THAN MANY SCORPIOS, BUT THIS WILL NOT
PREVENT YOU FROM TAKING ASSERTIVE ACTION WHEN NECESSARY.

Both Scorpio and Pisces belong to the water element and, as a result, there is a very natural sympathy between the two signs.

Self-expression
You have extremely powerful instincts and intuition, and should follow these. You also have an active imagination, and this, too, can work positively for you. However, if your imagination is operating negatively, you are capable of supposing that all sorts of things have gone wrong when, in fact, they probably have not. Try to avoid this by finding rewarding ways of expressing your imagination.

It may be that you have psychic ability. If you have premonitions or if strange things seem to happen to you from time to time, do not be worried. If, however, you want to develop your psychic powers, get special training from a psychic society of some kind. You have a powerful emotional level, and may often be swayed by your emotions. This need not be a negative trait, as long as you listen to your intuition, which will guide you in the direction that you should take.

Romance
You will get much pleasure from your love and sex life, and can give a great deal of yourself to your partners. However, you can be easily hurt and, if this occurs, it may be because you have not faced up to reality.

Your well-being
The Piscean body area covers the feet. Yours are vulnerable, and you probably find it difficult to get really comfortable shoes.

Many people with a Piscean emphasis tend to put on weight relatively easily, and Scorpios love good food. It is better for you to discipline your eating habits than to go on a crash diet.

The Moon in Pisces

Planning ahead

Although your Scorpio Sun gives you a good basic financial sense, your Piscean Moon succeeds in removing rather a lot of it. You have such a sensitivity to suffering, and identify so strongly with it, that you may be over-generous to charities. It could be that you also tend to lend money far too freely. Avoid this whenever possible, and remember that it is usually much better to give a few pounds to someone than to loan them money.

You should probably take financial advice when you are thinking of investing. Should you want to start a business, it is advisable for you to work with a partner, unless you feel that you really can control your Moon in Pisces soft approach to finance.

Parenthood

You are likely to have a great understanding of human nature, and it could well be of enormous help to you in your relationship with your children. You will sometimes be very strict with them, and at others times may tend to spoil them. If you manage to succeed in keeping these two extremes in balance, you will be a splendid parent.

MOON CHARTS

REFER TO THE FOLLOWING TABLES TO DISCOVER YOUR MOON SIGN.
THE PRECEDING PAGES WILL TELL YOU ABOUT ITS QUALITIES.

By referring to the Moon charts opposite and overleaf, look up the year of your birth and the Zodiacal glyph for your birth month. Refer next to the Moon Table (*below, left*) in which the days of the month are listed against a number. The number against the day of the month in which you were born indicates how many Zodiacal glyphs (*below, right*) must be counted before you reach your Moon sign. You may have to count to Pisces and return to Aries. For example, given the birthdate 21 May 1991, you initially need to find the Moon sign

for the first day of May in that year. It is Sagittarius ($\nearrow$). With the birthdate falling on the 21st, nine signs must be added. The Moon sign for this birth date is therefore Virgo ($\mathrm{I\!I\!\Omega}$).

Note that because the Moon moves so quickly, it is beyond the scope of this little book to provide a detailed chart of its positions. For more detailed horoscopes, consult an astrologer, but if you feel that this chart gives a result that does not seem to apply to you, read the pages for the signs either before or after the one indicated; one of the three will apply.

MOON TABLE

DAYS OF THE MONTH AND NUMBER OF SIGNS THAT SHOULD BE ADDED

DAY	ADD	DAY	ADD	DAY	ADD	DAY	ADD
1	0	9	4	17	7	25	11
2	1	10	4	18	8	26	11
3	1	11	5	19	8	27	12
4	1	12	5	20	9	28	12
5	2	13	5	21	9	29	1
6	2	14	6	22	10	30	1
7	3	15	6	23	10	31	2
8	3	16	7	24	10		

ZODIACAL GLYPHS

Ψ	Aries
$\eth$	Taurus
$\mathrm{I\!I}$	Gemini
$\mathfrak{S}$	Cancer
Ω	Leo
$\mathrm{I\!I\!\Omega}$	Virgo
$\triangle$	Libra
$\mathrm{I\!I\!\!\downarrow}$	Scorpio
$\nearrow$	Sagittarius
$\mathrm{V\!\!\!S}$	Capricorn
$\approx$	Aquarius
$\mathcal{H}$	Pisces

	1923	1924	1925	1926	1927	1928	1929	1930	1931	1932	1933	1934	1935
JAN	♊	♏	♈	♌	♐	♈	♍	♑	♉	♎	♓	♋	♏
FEB	♌	♐	♉	♍	♑	♊	♏	♓	♋	♐	♈	♌	♑
MAR	♌	♑	♉	♍	♒	♋	♏	♓	♋	♐	♉	♍	♑
APR	♎	♓	♋	♏	♈	♍	♑	♉	♍	♒	♊	♎	♓
MAY	♏	♈	♌	♐	♉	♎	♒	♊	♎	♓	♋	♐	♈
JUN	♑	♉	♍	♒	♋	♏	♓	♌	♐	♉	♍	♑	♊
JUL	♒	♋	♏	♓	♌	♐	♈	♍	♑	♊	♎	♓	♋
AUG	♈	♌	♐	♉	♍	♒	♊	♏	♓	♋	♐	♈	♌
SEP	♉	♎	♒	♋	♏	♓	♌	♐	♈	♍	♑	♊	♎
OCT	♊	♏	♓	♌	♐	♉	♍	♑	♉	♎	♓	♋	♏
NOV	♌	♑	♉	♍	♑	♉	♏	♓	♋	♐	♈	♌	♑
DEC	♍	♒	♊	♎	♓	♌	♐	♈	♌	♑	♉	♍	♒

	1936	1937	1938	1939	1940	1941	1942	1943	1944	1945	1946	1947	1948
JAN	♈	♌	♑	♉	♍	♒	♊	♎	♓	♌	♐	♈	♍
FEB	♉	♎	♒	♊	♏	♈	♌	♐	♉	♍	♑	♊	♎
MAR	♊	♎	♒	♋	♐	♈	♌	♐	♉	♎	♒	♊	♏
APR	♌	♐	♈	♌	♑	♉	♎	♒	♋	♏	♓	♌	♑
MAY	♍	♑	♉	♎	♒	♊	♏	♓	♌	♐	♉	♍	♒
JUN	♎	♒	♋	♏	♈	♌	♑	♉	♎	♒	♊	♏	♓
JUL	♏	♈	♌	♑	♉	♍	♒	♊	♏	♓	♌	♐	♈
AUG	♑	♉	♎	♒	♋	♏	♈	♌	♐	♉	♍	♑	♊
SEP	♓	♋	♏	♈	♌	♑	♉	♍	♒	♋	♏	♓	♌
OCT	♈	♌	♑	♉	♎	♒	♊	♎	♓	♌	♐	♈	♍
NOV	♊	♎	♒	♊	♏	♈	♌	♐	♉	♍	♑	♊	♏
DEC	♋	♏	♓	♌	♑	♉	♍	♑	♊	♎	♒	♋	♐

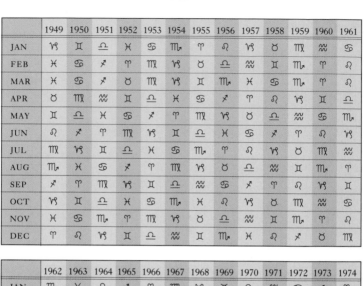

	1949	1950	1951	1952	1953	1954	1955	1956	1957	1958	1959	1960	1961
JAN	♑	♊	♎	♓	♋	♏	♈	♌	♑	♉	♍	♒	♋
FEB	♓	♋	♐	♈	♍	♑	♉	♎	♒	♊	♏	♈	♌
MAR	♓	♋	♐	♉	♍	♑	♊	♏	♓	♋	♏	♈	♌
APR	♉	♍	♒	♊	♎	♓	♋	♐	♈	♌	♑	♊	♎
MAY	♊	♎	♓	♋	♐	♈	♍	♑	♉	♎	♒	♋	♏
JUN	♌	♐	♈	♍	♑	♊	♎	♓	♋	♐	♈	♌	♑
JUL	♍	♑	♊	♎	♓	♋	♏	♈	♌	♑	♉	♍	♒
AUG	♏	♓	♋	♐	♈	♍	♑	♉	♎	♒	♊	♏	♈
SEP	♐	♈	♍	♑	♊	♎	♒	♋	♐	♈	♌	♑	♊
OCT	♑	♊	♎	♓	♋	♏	♓	♌	♑	♉	♍	♒	♋
NOV	♓	♋	♏	♈	♍	♑	♉	♎	♒	♊	♏	♈	♌
DEC	♈	♌	♑	♊	♎	♒	♊	♏	♓	♌	♐	♉	♍

	1962	1963	1964	1965	1966	1967	1968	1969	1970	1971	1972	1973	1974
JAN	♏	♓	♌	♐	♈	♍	♑	♊	♎	♒	♋	♐	♈
FEB	♐	♉	♍	♒	♊	♏	♓	♋	♏	♈	♍	♑	♉
MAR	♐	♉	♎	♒	♊	♏	♈	♌	♐	♉	♍	♑	♊
APR	♒	♋	♏	♈	♌	♑	♉	♍	♒	♊	♏	♓	♋
MAY	♓	♌	♐	♉	♍	♒	♊	♎	♓	♋	♐	♈	♍
JUN	♉	♎	♒	♊	♏	♓	♌	♐	♉	♍	♑	♊	♎
JUL	♊	♏	♓	♌	♐	♈	♍	♑	♊	♎	♓	♋	♐
AUG	♌	♐	♉	♎	♒	♊	♏	♓	♋	♏	♈	♍	♑
SEP	♍	♒	♋	♏	♓	♋	♐	♉	♍	♑	♊	♎	♓
OCT	♏	♓	♌	♐	♈	♍	♒	♊	♎	♒	♋	♐	♈
NOV	♐	♉	♎	♒	♊	♏	♓	♋	♐	♈	♍	♑	♉
DEC	♑	♊	♏	♓	♋	♐	♈	♌	♑	♉	♎	♒	♊

58

	1975	1976	1977	1978	1979	1980	1981	1982	1983	1984	1985	1986	1987
JAN	♌	♑	♉	♍	♒	♊	♏	♓	♌	♐	♉	♍	♑
FEB	♎	♒	♋	♏	♈	♌	♐	♉	♍	♒	♊	♎	♓
MAR	♎	♓	♋	♏	♈	♍	♑	♉	♎	♒	♊	♏	♓
APR	♐	♈	♍	♑	♊	♎	♒	♋	♏	♈	♌	♑	♉
MAY	♑	♉	♎	♒	♋	♏	♓	♌	♐	♉	♍	♒	♊
JUN	♓	♋	♐	♈	♌	♑	♉	♎	♒	♊	♏	♓	♌
JUL	♈	♌	♑	♉	♍	♒	♋	♏	♓	♌	♐	♉	♍
AUG	♉	♎	♓	♋	♏	♈	♌	♐	♈	♎	♒	♊	♎
SEP	♋	♐	♈	♌	♐	♊	♎	♒	♊	♏	♓	♌	♐
OCT	♌	♑	♉	♍	♒	♋	♏	♓	♋	♐	♉	♍	♑
NOV	♎	♓	♋	♏	♓	♌	♐	♉	♍	♒	♊	♎	♓
DEC	♏	♈	♌	♐	♉	♍	♑	♓	♎	♓	♋	♐	♈

	1988	1989	1990	1991	1992	1993	1994	1995	1996	1997	1998	1999	2000
JAN	♊	♎	♒	♋	♏	♈	♌	♑	♉	♎	♒	♊	♏
FEB	♋	♐	♈	♍	♑	♉	♎	♒	♋	♏	♈	♌	♐
MAR	♌	♐	♉	♍	♒	♊	♎	♓	♋	♏	♈	♌	♑
APR	♍	♒	♊	♏	♓	♋	♐	♈	♍	♑	♊	♎	♓
MAY	♏	♓	♌	♐	♈	♍	♑	♉	♎	♒	♋	♏	♈
JUN	♐	♉	♍	♑	♊	♎	♓	♋	♐	♈	♌	♑	♉
JUL	♑	♊	♎	♒	♋	♐	♈	♌	♑	♉	♎	♒	♋
AUG	♓	♌	♐	♈	♍	♑	♉	♎	♓	♋	♏	♓	♌
SEP	♉	♍	♑	♊	♏	♓	♋	♏	♈	♌	♑	♉	♎
OCT	♊	♎	♒	♋	♐	♈	♌	♑	♉	♎	♒	♊	♏
NOV	♌	♐	♈	♍	♑	♉	♎	♒	♋	♏	♈	♌	♑
DEC	♍	♑	♉	♎	♒	♋	♏	♈	♌	♐	♉	♍	♒

THE
SOLAR SYSTEM

THE STARS, OTHER THAN THE SUN, PLAY NO PART IN THE SCIENCE
OF ASTROLOGY. ASTROLOGERS USE ONLY THE BODIES IN THE
SOLAR SYSTEM, EXCLUDING THE EARTH, TO CALCULATE HOW OUR
LIVES AND PERSONALITIES CHANGE.

Pluto
Pluto takes 246 years to travel around
the Sun. It affects our unconscious
instincts and urges, gives us strength
in difficulty, and perhaps emphasizes
any inherent cruel streak.

Neptune
Neptune stays in each sign for 14
years. At best it makes us sensitive
and imaginative; at worst it
encourages deceit and carelessness,
making us worry.

Uranus
Uranus's influence can make us
friendly, kind, eccentric, inventive,
and unpredictable.

Saturn
In ancient times, Saturn was the most
distant known planet. Its influence
can limit our ambition and make us
either overly cautious (but practical),
or reliable and self-disciplined.

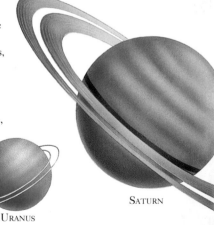

PLUTO

NEPTUNE

URANUS

SATURN

Jupiter

Jupiter encourages expansion, optimism, generosity, and breadth of vision. It can, however, also make us wasteful, extravagant, and conceited.

Mars

Much associated with energy, anger, violence, selfishness, and a strong sex drive, Mars also encourages decisiveness and leadership.

JUPITER

The Moon

Although it is a satellite of the Earth, the Moon is known in astrology as a planet. It lies about 240,000 miles from the Earth and, astrologically, is second in importance to the Sun.

THE MOON

MERCURY

VENUS

EARTH

MARS

The Sun

The Sun, the only star used by astrologers, influences the way we present ourselves to the world – our image or personality; the "us" we show to other people.

Venus

The planet of love and partnership, Venus can emphasize all our best personal qualities. It may also encourage us to be lazy, impractical, and too dependent on other people.

Earth

Every planet contributes to the environment of the Solar System, and a person born on Venus would no doubt be influenced by our own planet in some way.

Mercury

The planet closest to the Sun affects our intellect. It can make us inquisitive, versatile, argumentative, perceptive, and clever, but maybe also inconsistent, cynical, and sarcastic.